Food

BREAD

Louise Spilsbury

Heinemann
LIBRARY

www.heinemann.co.uk/library
Visit our website to find out more information about Heinemann Library books.

To order:
☎ Phone 44 (0) 1865 888066
🖹 Send a fax to 44 (0) 1865 314091
🖥 Visit the Heinemann Bookshop at www.heinemann.co.uk/library to browse our catalogue and order online.

First published in Great Britain by Heinemann Library,
Halley Court, Jordan Hill, Oxford OX2 8EJ
a division of Reed Educational and Professional Publishing Ltd.
Heinemann is a registered trademark of Reed Educational & Professional Publishing Ltd.

OXFORD MELBOURNE AUCKLAND
JOHANNESBURG BLANTYRE GABORONE
IBADAN PORTSMOUTH (NH) USA CHICAGO

Designed by Celia Floyd
Illustrated by Barry Atkinson
Originated by Ambassador Litho Ltd
Printed by South China Printing Co in Hong Kong.

ISBN 0 431 12700 X
05 04 03 02 01
10 9 8 7 6 5 4 3 2 1

0431 127 00X 4409
X 000 000 044 1409

British Library Cataloguing in Publication Data
Spilsbury, Louise
  Bread. – (Food)
  1. Bread 2. Cookery (Bread)
  I. Title
  641.8'15

641.815

Acknowledgements
The Publishers would like to thank the following for permission to reproduce photographs:
Anthony Blake pp.6, 8, 10, 15; APV Bakers pp. 15, 16, 17, 18; Gareth Boden pp. 7, 22, 23, 25, 28, 29; Bridgeman/Fitzwilliam Museum, University of Cambridge p.9; Britstock p.19, 20; Corbis p.11; Bruce Coleman p.12; Food Features p.14; Robert Harding p.21; Photodisc/H Wiesenhofer/PhotoLink p.5; Photoshop/Trevor Clifford p.4; Tony Stone Images/Lori Adamski Peek p.24.

Cover photograph reproduced with permission of Gareth Boden.

Every effort has been made to contact copyright holders of any material reproduced in this book. Any omissions will be rectified in subsequent printings if notice is given to the Publisher.

CONTENTS

Words written in bold, **like this**, are explained in the Glossary.

WHAT IS BREAD?

Bread is a very important food. Lots of people eat bread two or three times a day. There are many different kinds of bread.

All breads are made from **flour** and water. Flour is made from the **grains** of **cereal** plants. Most of the bread we eat is made from a plant called **wheat**. These are wheat plants.

KINDS OF BREAD

Breads taste different when they are made with different kinds of **flour**. This yellow cornbread from America is made with **corn** flour, also called maize flour.

Rye flour makes dark bread with a strong taste. Rye flour is used to make crispbreads and rye bread like these.

IN THE PAST

People have been eating bread for around 5000 years. The first breads were made from just **flour** and water. They were flat breads a bit like these.

The **Egyptians** found a way of making bread with **yeast** in it. Yeast makes bread bigger and full of air. This model shows Egyptians making bread about 4000 years ago.

AROUND THE WORLD

People eat flat breads in many countries around the world. Indian chapatis are made from **wheat flour** and water.

In France people eat many kinds of bread. Many French people eat bread with every meal. Long, crusty loaves called baguettes are very popular. We often call them French sticks.

LOOKING AT WHEAT

Most bread is made from **wheat flour**. Wheat flour is made by **grinding** the **grains** from a wheat plant into a powder. These are wheat plants.

grains

stalk

leaf

Flour made from the **endosperm** (the inside) is used to make white bread. Brown flour is a mix of white flour and **bran**. **Wholemeal** flour is made from the whole wheat grain. This is a grain of wheat.

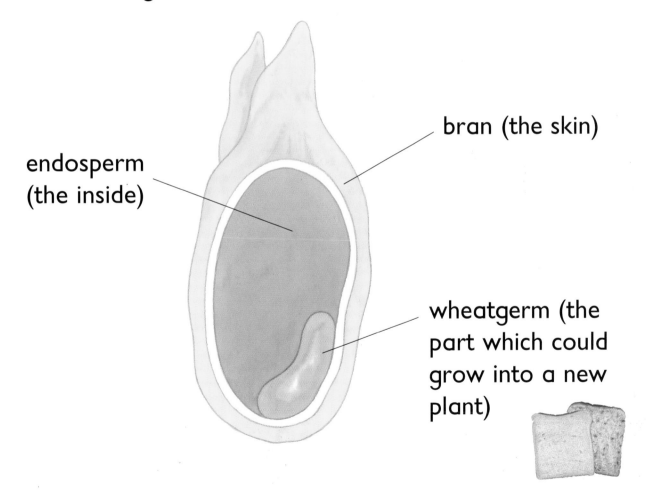

endosperm (the inside)

bran (the skin)

wheatgerm (the part which could grow into a new plant)

WHERE IS BREAD MADE?

Some people buy bread fresh every day from a bakery, and some people still make bread at home. The bread most people eat is made in large **factory** bakeries.

In a factory bakery, people use machines to make bread. First the **ingredients** are measured out. Usually these are **flour**, water, salt and **yeast**.

MAKING BREAD

The **flour**, salt, water and **yeast** are put into a large container. A very fast machine mixes them together until they form a smooth, soft **dough**.

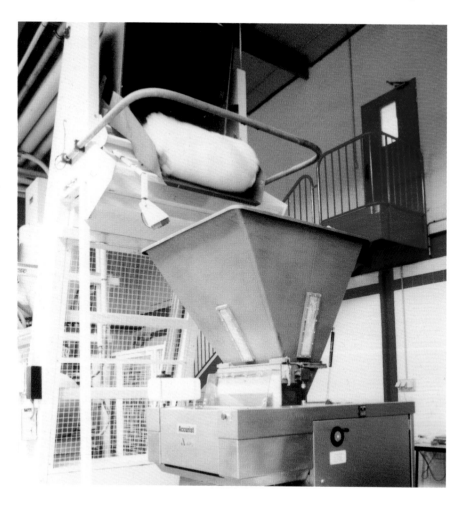

Then a machine cuts the dough into pieces of the same size and weight. It carries the cut pieces of dough along on a **conveyor belt**.

PROVING AND BAKING

The machine drops the dough into tins. The **conveyor belt** takes them to a 'proving area'. This is a warm place where they stay until the **yeast** starts working and the loaves rise.

Then the conveyor belt moves
the loaves into a very hot oven.
A computer checks that they bake
for just the right amount of time.

SLICING AND PACKING

After the loaves have cooled down, they are taken out of the tins. The **conveyor belt** takes some loaves to the sharp knives that make them into sliced bread.

Then the bread is put into packets.
Labels tell **consumers** what is in the
bread and how long it will stay fresh.

EATING BREAD

People eat bread on its own, with soup or to make many different kinds of sandwiches. You can make sandwiches from fresh or toasted bread.

People make toast by **grilling** bread in a toaster or a grill. They put butter or margarine and other spreads, like jam, on top.

GOOD FOR YOU

Bread is a **carbohydrate**. This means it is a kind of food that gives you **energy**. We use up energy in everything we do.

Wholemeal bread is better for you than white bread. It contains **nutrients** and **fibre**. These things help to keep your body healthy.

HEALTHY EATING

You need to eat different kinds of food to keep well. This food pyramid shows how much of each different food you need.

Bread is in the group of foods at the bottom of the pyramid. You need to eat some of the things in that group every day.

You should eat some of the foods shown in the middle every day, too. You need only small amounts of the foods at the top.

The food in each part of the pyramid helps your body in different ways.

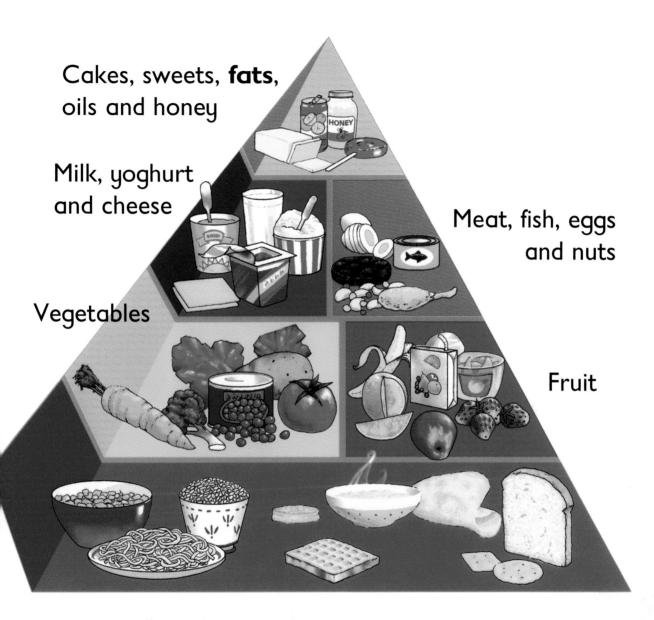

Cakes, sweets, **fats**, oils and honey

Milk, yoghurt and cheese

Meat, fish, eggs and nuts

Vegetables

Fruit

Bread, **cereals**, rice and pasta

EGGY BREAD RECIPE

1 Break the egg into a bowl and mix with a fork.

2 Add the milk and mix. Now pour the mixture onto a large plate.

You will need:
- 1 egg
- 1 dessertspoon milk
- butter
- 2 slices bread

Ask an adult to help you!

3 Spread a little butter on the slices of bread. Dip them in the egg mix.

4 Put the bread onto a baking tray. Cook in a hot oven for 5 minutes, or until brown.

5 Eat with jam or fruit.

GLOSSARY

bran brown skin around a grain of wheat

carbohydrates nutrients from the food we eat that give us energy

cereal grains such as wheat, rye, corn and rice that are used to make foods like flour, bread and breakfast cereals

consumers people who buy things that they need or want, like food

conveyor belt moving belt which takes things from one place to another in a factory

corn cereal plant (also called maize). Corn grains are yellow.

dough soft, thick mixture made with flour and water

Egyptians the Ancient Egyptians ruled over many lands around 4000 years ago. They are famous for their great buildings, their farms and their writing.

endosperm inside of a grain of wheat

energy all living things need energy to live, move and grow. Our energy comes from the food we eat.

factory very big building where people and machines make things such as shoes or toys, or foods such as bread

fats type of food. Butter, oil and margarine are types of fat. It is not healthy to eat too many fatty foods.

fibre part of a plant that passes through our bodies when we eat it. As it does this, it helps to keep our bodies healthy.

flour powder made by grinding the grains of cereal plants. Cereal plants used to make flour include wheat, rye and maize.

grains seeds of a cereal plant

grilling when food is cooked using direct heat from above or below

grinding crushing grains into a powder

ingredients kinds of food, such as flour and water, cooked together to make another food

nutrients goodness in food that we need to stay healthy

rye cereal plant. The grains of the rye plant can be used to make flour.

wheat cereal plant. The grain (seed) of the wheat plant is ground to make flour for cooking.

wholemeal wholemeal flour is made from the whole wheat grain

yeast tiny living plants. When mixed with warm water, yeast makes bubbles of gas. This makes the bread rise (puff out).

31

MORE BOOKS TO READ

Plants: Plants and Us, Angela Royston, Heinemann Library, 1999

Bodywise: Why Do I Feel Hungry? Sharon Cromwell, Heinemann Library, 1998

Senses: Tasting, Karen Hartley, Chris Macro, Philip Taylor, Heinemann Library, 2000

What's for Lunch? Bread Franklin Watts

INDEX

Titles in the *Food* series include:

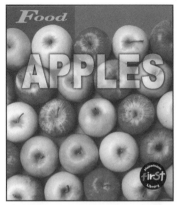

Hardback   0 431 12708 5

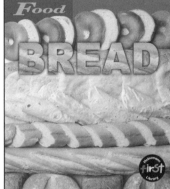

Hardback   0 431 12700 X

Hardback   0 431 12702 6

Hardback   0 431 12706 9

Hardback   0 431 12701 8

Hardback   0 431 12703 4

Hardback   0 431 12707 7

Hardback   0 431 12705 0

Find out about the other titles in this series on our website www.heinemann.co.uk/library